Brixton Stories
&
Happy Birthday, Mister Deka D

Biyi Bandele's plays include *Marching For Fausa* (Royal Court), *Two Horsemen* (Gate/Bush), *Resurrections* (Talawa at the Cochrane Theatre), *Death Catches the Hunter* (Wild Iris tour/BAC), *Thieves Like Us* (Southwark Playhouse and Radio 4), *Things Fall Apart* (LIFT/Royal Court and Radio 4), *Happy Birthday, Mister Deka D* (Edinburgh Festival, Lyric Hammersmith), *Yerma* (Chipping Norton Theatre/Fifth Amendment) and *Aphra Behn's Oroonoko* (RSC). Film screenplays include: *Ways of Dying* Skreba/British Screen), *Not Even God is Wise Enough* (BBC). He has written three novels: *The Man who Came in From the Back of Beyond*, *The Sympathetic Undertaker and Other Dreams* and *The Street* upon which *Brixton Stories* is based. Biyi Bandele was the 2000–1 Judith E. Wilson fellow at Churchill College, Cambridge University. He was born in Nigeria and now lives in London.

Brixton Stories

or

The Short and Happy Life of Ossie Jones

&
Happy Birthday, Mister Deka D

Biyi Bandele

Methuen Drama

Published by Methuen 2001

1 3 5 7 9 10 8 6 4 2

First published in 2001 by
Methuen Publishing Limited,
215 Vauxhall Bridge Road,
London SW1V 1EJ

Copyright © Biyi Bandele 2001

The right of Biyi Bandele to be identified as the author of these works
has been asserted by him in accordance with the Copyright,
Designs and Patents Act, 1988

Methuen Publishing Limited Reg. No. 3543167

A CIP catalogue record for this book is available from the British Library

ISBN 0 413 77181 4

Typeset by SX Composing DTP, Rayleigh, Essex
Printed and bound in Great Britain by
Cox & Wyman Ltd, Reading, Berkshire

Caution

Contents

Brixton Stories   1

Happy Birthday, Mister Deka D   45

Brixton Stories

Brixton Stories was first performed at the Tricycle Theatre, London, 17 October 2001. This play was originally performed as a workshop production in the RSC's The Other Eden season, The Pit Theatre, London, 11 April 2001. The performers were:

Judy Akuwudike
Diane Parrish

Directed by Roxana Silbert
Designed by Niki Turner

Spotlight rises on Ossie Jones as he gets ready to go to bed. And on Nehushta, who is fast asleep in another room.

Ossie   On the night Ossie Jones died, just before he drifted into the deep sleep out of which he would not emerge, he thought of his wife, Kate, whose spitting image, their daughter, Nehushta, had kissed him good night half an hour earlier and –

A voice off-stage suddenly crashes in. It is coming from the **Neighbour Upstairs**.

Neighbour Upstairs (*off*)   And when I go to court I said to de judge – My Lord, I 'ave already did smoke de cannabis but it's in me body and I don't have none!

Ossie   That's the neighbour upstairs.

Neighbour Upstairs   Me say yes, me admit to guilt to say me did smoke it, I must tell you de truth. But I only smoke me little ganja, and do me little carpentry work.

Nehushta *bangs on the ceiling.*

Ossie (*wryly*)   That's Nehushta – talking to the neighbour upstairs.

He pauses, primed for further interruptions. There are none.

On the night Ossie Jones died, he thought of many things.

He pauses, as if trying to remember.

He thought of the slouching shadows of lonesome giants and the radiance of a shared moment, the syncopated silence of selective amnesia and the resonating infinitude of a done deed, the ticking of time and the hypothesis of immortality, the threat of rain and the beauty of a green landscape, the falling out of teeth and the serenity of a toothless smile, the numbing shock of a sudden disappointment and the lingering scream into which an orgasm erupts.

Ossie *crawls into bed and goes to sleep.*

Nehushta   Sometime during the night, Ossie's daughter, Nehushta, suddenly woke up to a deep thirst. She got up, half-asleep, and headed for the kitchen.

She gets up, half-asleep, and heads for the kitchen.

As she went across the living room, which she had to go through to reach the kitchen –

She sees **Ossie**, *now fast asleep on his sofa bed.*

She glanced briefly at Ossie and smiled because he looked so at peace. She tripped over something which, when she opened her eyes wide and was properly awake, turned out to be a thin strip of light that had wandered into the room through the slits in the blinds from the street lamps outside. She pulled the blinds aside and looked out on to the street. The weather had taken an unseasonably foggy turn.

She tenses.

A strange sense of foreboding came over her. She stood very still.

She stands still. Holds her breath.

Dad? (*Moves towards him.*) Dad!

She holds him, checking for signs of life.

As Ossie Jones crept out of his body and into the mist, his heart murmured till it was silent.

She shuts his eyes and cries quietly.

As lights rise fully, we are transported to the outdoors, to the streets.

Nehushta   It seemed such a long time ago now, when earlier that day, they had walked along the streets of Brixton, arm in arm, father and daughter, as if without a care in the world –

Ossie (*getting up*)   – Surrounded by the ever-present floating cast of the walking wounded and the clinically Undead –

The performer playing **Nehushta** *becomes a member of the Brixton Undead: cigarette in one hand, a can of Special Brew in the other, a baseball cap worn backwards, and a handwritten sign hanging from his neck that says: 'Wife, three children and two dogs to keep. please help.'*

Ossie   Damaged souls haunted by memories of past transgressions and paralysed with guilt for sins not yet committed –

The performer playing **Nehushta** *becomes a strung-out junkie in the grips of a catatonic high.*

Ossie   Mavens, gurus, roshis, lamas, shamans, revolutionaries, avatars, seers, illuminati, diviners, prognosticators, prophets and those who considered themselves the street clerisy, and who posed questions such as –

Soapbox Philosopher   'Where does the light go when you cut the switch off?'

Ossie   And – *(turns expectantly to the* **Soapbox Philosopher***)* – answered it.

Soapbox Philosopher *looks blankly at him.*

Nehushta   There were also the *Big Issue* vendors –

The performer playing Ossie becomes a ***Big Issue*** **Vendor**.

Big Issue **Vendor**
    'Biggie, Biggie, Biggie!
    Float like a butterfly, sting like a bee-gie
    Your hands can't hit what your eyes can't see-gie
    So, stop right now and buy a *Biggie!*'

Nehushta   And the busker who spent half an hour mimicking the sounds of gunshots and police sirens, which he humbly offered as –

Busker *(with an East European accent)*   The Brixton national anthem, ladies and gentlemen. *(Passing his hat around, faultlessly polite.)* Do please be generous, ladies and gentlemen. This is how I make my living. I don't get money from the government or any other criminal organisation. Thank you all and God bless you.

Nehushta   And the two men, both so drunk they could only stay on their feet by hanging on to each other (only two hours earlier, at the Beehive public house, they'd been total strangers) . . .

The two performers become the two drunken men, an **Ethiopian** *and a* **Jamaican**, *swaying gently, unsteadily, on their feet.*

Ethiopian   Have you ever studied in your life?

Jamaican (*bristles*)   Cos I have, man. I did paintin'.

Ethiopian (*unimpressed*)   What is dat?

Jamaican   Paintin', just paintin'. Paintin' woodwork, doors, walls.

Ethiopian (*unconvinced*)   That's not studyin'.

Jamaican   Yes, man, cos it is. You can take a course in paintin', ain't it?

Ethiopian (*adamantly*)   That's not studyin'.

Jamaican   No? You can paint? You can paint? Let me tell you something, can you start a work? Can you rub down a wall, fill it up, paint it and finish it? Can you do dat? Can you fill up every nook and cranny, and all dat make de house look like it brand new?

Ethiopian   I can. Only not perfect.

Jamaican (*triumphantly*)   Not perfect! Well, let me tell you something, I can come to your flat and I can say dere needs fillin' up, dere needs fillin' up, what a big hole! – You kna a mean – paintin' is no simple ting you know. Anybody could dip a brush in a bloody paint pot and slap it on de wall. Yeah. But you have to go through de preparation. You have to go through the preparation, dat's what I say.

Ethiopian (*in all earnestness*)   What I want is a grant, to help me to do what I want to do.

Jamaican   What is it you want to do?

Ethiopian   Finish my studyin'. My electronic study. I need to dress.

Jamaican (*quizzically*)   What are you studyin'?

Ethiopian (*matter-of-fact*)   Electronic.

Jamaican   You don't need to dress up to do electronics!

The two drunks lapse into silence.

Nehushta   Ossie and his daughter also stopped briefly to browse through the wares of Mr Bill, the wordmonger of Brixton, who was to be found every weekday during the morning rush hour sitting outside the tube station, touching commuters for money by enacting one or more of his specialities which included reciting and offering –

Wordmonger   The meanings, origins, synonyms, antonymns and, where applicable, usage and abusage of every single word under the letter H in the *Oxford English Dictionary*.

Nehushta   He would even throw in the homonyms, his ulcers permitting. But that was in winter. In the summer Mr Bill sold words for a living. He would take his usual spot outside the station, beside the newsagent's stall, and sitting there he would whisper words into the ears of passers-by –

Wordmonger (*Using the audience for passers-by, plies his trade, softly.*) Tintinnabulation, discombobulate, serendipity . . .

Nehushta   – for a modest fee, the average being –

Wordmonger   Ten pence, please. Ten pence per word.

Nehushta   Though some had been known to buy whole sentences.

Wordmonger   One man bought a paragraph. It was a birthday gift for his wife.

Nehushta   Others simply came back for more words. One woman bought three words –

Wordmonger   Then returned the following day to ask for a refund.

Nehushta   Courteous as ever Mr Bill said –

Wordmonger   Very well, madam, may I have my words back?

Nehushta   The woman stamped her foot in fury: she'd forgotten the first word –

Wordmonger   She couldn't pronounce the second –

Nehushta   And the third had escaped through her nose when she – (*sneezes*)

Ossie   – from a bad cold.

Nehushta   Mr Bill took pity on her and gave her –

Wordmonger   Three new words free of charge. (*Checks, with a magnifying glass.*) One had been damaged in transit and suffered from – (*checks again*) – a fractured syllable.

Nehushta   So he replaced it with another word. The woman was speechless with gratitude –

Nehushta/Speechless *speechless with gratitude.*

Nehushta   Later that day, in the quiet of his bunk under Waterloo Bridge, he repaired the broken word with –

Wordmonger (*repairing it*)   A needle and thread –

Nehushta   It was the best he could do. The needle pierced his finger –

Wordmonger (*in genuine pain*)   – Aarrrgh! –

Nehushta   He was seen once on Portobello Road haggling with a second-hand word merchant over the wholesale price of a mouthful of words.

Ossie   He got them cheaply –

Nehushta   They'd been damaged by rain. He laid them out in the sun to dry. One of the words had suffered a broken wrist –

Ossie   Which had healed into a fist unable to open.

Nehushta   The wordmonger nursed it back to health: it shook hands and opened doors and warmed itself before a fire and waved at friends going away.

Ossie   He'd been spotted twice on Oxford Street going through rubbish bins for stray, homeless or discarded words. A Chinese tourist, who took the Polaroid evidence back to Guangzhou to show her friends, captured him once on camera –

Nehushta   In Covent Garden performing an illusion with words.

Ossie (*demonstrates*)   He coughed out the words, which took the shape of his cigarette-stained teeth turned into birds bereft of wing. He stammered the bloodied words into the palm of his hand, polished them into clearness –

Nehushta   With a stainless handkerchief –

Ossie   And gifted them with wings, and sent them flying into the great void beyond sound or silence, where all words uttered in the universe, and in all languages are stored for all time –

Nehushta   Or forgotten forever.

The performer playing **Ossie** *steps on top of an improvised soapbox and immediately transforms into a Bible-wielding, brimstone-and-fire evangelist whom we shall call the* **Preacher**.

Preacher　My face is set, my gait is fast, my goal is heaven, my road is narrow, my way rough, my companions few, my guide reliable, my mission clear. I cannot be bought, compromised, detoured, lured away, turned back, deluded, or delayed. I will not flinch in the face of sacrifice, hesitate in the presence of the adversary, negotiate at the table of the enemy, pander at the pool of popularity, or meander in the maze of mediocrity. I won't give up, shut up, let up, until I have stayed up, stored up, prayed up, paid up, and preached up for the cause of Jesus Christ!

Ossie (*to* **Nehushta**)　Who on earth is he?

Nehushta　He –

Preacher (*in mid-sentence*)　That's our problem! We can't do anything ourselves in order to deal with the problem. We are utterly unable to do anything. God – (*gestures skywards*) God did it for us!

The performer playing **Nehushta** *becomes the* **Heckler**.

Heckler　Don't point! We know where your finger's been.

We have met the **Heckler** *before. He is the man with a cigarette in one hand, a can of Special Brew in the other, a baseball cap worn backwards, and a hand-written sign hanging from his neck that says: 'Wife, three children and two dogs to keep. Please help.'*

Preacher　The Lord Jesus Christ left Heaven –

Heckler　He didn't leave Heaven, he left a gay discotheque.

Preacher (*ignores the* **Heckler**)　The Lord Jesus Christ left Heaven, came into this world, went to the cross . . . he was put on trial, and at this trial the judge said he was innocent. The Bible says he was tempted in every way like we are, yet he was without sin!

Heckler　I'll have sin and tonic!

Preacher　No one could accuse him rightly. Everyone who encountered him had to acknowledge –

Heckler   What would have happened in Bethlehem if Mary had used contraceptives?

Preacher   – Nicodemus, leader of the day, totally uninterested in spiritual things, had to say to Jesus Christ, 'No one could do the things you do, unless he'd been sent from God.'

Heckler   What would have happened that night if the Holy Ghost, when he descended upon Mary, had been wearing a condom?

The **Preacher**, *thrown off his train of thought, pauses briefly.*

Heckler (*triumphantly*)   There would have been no Jesus!

Preacher (*regains his composure*)   Jesus lived a sinless life. He went to death on the cross so that we could be made right. So that we could know forgiveness from sin.

Heckler (*derisively*)   I bet the Holy Ghost didn't find Mary's G-spot.

Preacher (*getting quite irritated*)   I'm not talking about a laugh and a joke on Brixton High Street. I'm talking about something tangible.

Heckler   Yes, would you move the platform closer to that tree. Pity, the rope doesn't quite reach.

Preacher   The Lord Jesus Christ will come back from Heaven and take those who love him, those who know him . . . he will take them home to be with him in Heaven.

Heckler   Off you go!

Preacher   Ladies and gentlemen, you may laugh. You may joke –

Heckler   Look, mate, if Heaven's so wonderful, what the hell are you waiting for?

Preacher   – but one day, each of us has to stand before a God who's just, a God who's impartial –

Heckler   There's a bus leaving in five minutes.

Preacher   The Lord Jesus Christ, nailed down on the cross, took my sin, took your sin and had it laid upon himself. You must come like Pilgrim in *Pilgrim's Progress* –

Heckler   *Who?*

Preacher   – to the foot of the cross, to have your burden rolled away. Here, in Brixton's own mini Speaker's Corner, everyone who comes here has something to say . . .

Heckler   Yes, I have two words to say to you and the second one is 'off'!

Preacher   Whether they are a philosophy, whether they are a religion. Everyone is trying to point the way. Well, there is a very, very important question – when you're dead, you're done for. When you're six foot under, you're finished. But hang on a moment, folks, where do we go when we die?

Nehushta   This question from the preacher –

Preacher   Where do we go when we die?

Nehushta   This question, which she really had no strong opinions about, nevertheless took Nehushta's mind back to an incident that happened to Ossie a long time ago.

The street disappears and we are taken to **Ossie**'s *home.*

It was shortly after her thirteenth birthday. Ossie came home from work one evening looking more troubled than was usual for him. She knew that something was wrong.

Ossie   I saw my brother today.

Nehushta   He said when she asked him what was the matter.

Ossie   I saw Taiye at St Pancras.

Nehushta   Ever since Kate, Nehushta's mother, died Ossie had changed almost beyond recognition. A grey peninsula had evolved overnight on the tousled wilderness of his balding head. His eyes peeked out of their sockets, lonely and devoid of purpose, like lights shining into a great void revealing nothing but the darkness ahead. He was almost fully functional during weekdays. His workload as an immigration lawyer kept him busy and with no time to brood.

Ossie   The *difficult* we do immediately –

Nehushta   He comforted a client facing imminent deportation.

Ossie   But –

Nehushta   He added:

Ossie   – the *impossible* takes time to accomplish.

Nehushta   Weekends, though, he came home reeking of alcohol and all bandaged up.

Ossie   I've been walking into things –

Nehushta   He would say to his daughter.

Ossie   Lamp-posts – and pubs mostly.

Nehushta   When he came home that night looking agitated, Nehushta poured him a glass of whisky and watched him hurriedly knock it back.

Ossie (*holds out the glass for another tipple*)   I saw my brother today.

Nehushta (*gently*)   You couldn't have seen your brother, Dad. Your brother died twenty years ago.

Ossie   I know he died twenty years ago. Why else would I be so shaken. I swear, Nehushta. It was him, it was Taiye. (*To audience.*) She said nothing. She knew that nothing she said would make him change his mind. She poured him another drink.

Nehushta   Dad, I once heard you say to someone, you said, 'You cannot stop the birds of sorrow from flying over your head but you can prevent them from building nests in your beard.'

Ossie   I said that? God, I wonder what I'd been drinking.

Nehushta   And with that, he keeled over and fell asleep.

Ossie *keels over and falls asleep.*

Nehushta   Nehushta pulled off her father's shoes and half carried, half dragged him to his bedroom. She took off his tie and tucked him into bed. He was snoring loudly when she turned off the light and shut his bedroom door behind her.

Nehushta *exits.* **Ossie** *sleeps, snoring loudly.*

Ossie (*finally, rises*)   As his daughter switched off the light and shut the door behind her that night, Ossie Jones drifted from a deep, drunken sleep into a dream in which he was completely sober – (*getting into a 'car'*) – and in his car driving down a strange, liminal highway that stretched from a nebulous tunnel at the soles of his feet, past the toll gates of his soul, where he was stopped, even his passport checked, and into the boundless openness of the universe. (*Drives at high speed. Slows down.*) A vicious wind colluding with heavy rains transformed the journey into a blind, non-stop flight on a treacherously endless highway.

He slots a tape into the car stereo. He drives on for a while, listening to the music, letting it wash over him.

Then, all of a sudden, the engine stalls.

He gets out of the car, into the rain and opens the bonnet. He messes about with a few plugs but soon gives up after the stalled engine raises his hopes three times and three times dashes them against the hard shoulder.

He proceeded to attempt to cadge a lift. Several cars went by without stopping, but finally salvation appeared in the distance. Its headlights grew bigger and brighter and then it screeched to a halt. He was caught between the headlights, sepulchral, trapped within a halo of self-pity. The lights dimmed to reveal a limousine. The driver leaned out and shouted –

Apha *enters.*

Apha   Hurry up!

Ossie   It was a boy's voice, the voice of a young man. For a nanosecond Ossie stood frozen to the spot, paralysed by a certain dissonance, an inexplicable feeling of foreboding that took possession of him.

Apha (*impatiently*)   Hey, mister!

Ossie   Ossie hurried to the slightly open door, taking off his topcoat as he got into the car.

Apha (*chewing gum loudly*)   You can sling that in the back.

Ossie   The boy was, as Ossie had guessed from his voice, quite young; no older than sixteen.

Apha *offers him bubble gum.*

Ossie (*shaking his head*)   No, thanks.

Apha   You look tired. Are you tired?

Ossie   I am quite tired. Thanks for stopping for me. I'd been standing in that rain for nearly an hour.

Apha   Your car broke down.

Ossie   Yes.

Apha   Smoke?

Ossie   No. I don't smoke. Where were you coming from?

Apha   Here and there. You?

Ossie   London.

Apha   Yeah? (*Rolls the word in his mouth.*) 'London.' Where's that? (*Swerves.*)

Ossie *is not quite sure whether or not the boy is serious. But he is far too tired to respond.*

Ossie   Where are you going?

Apha   Nowhere in particular. Just taking the car for a spin.

Ossie   In this weather? At this hour?

Apha   I'm Apha. You are – ?

Ossie   Ossie. Ossie Jones.

Apha   I can't place your accent. Where are you from?

Ossie   Nigeria. But I've lived in England for –

Apha   Where's that?

Ossie   Nigeria?

Apha   That too. And the other place you just mentioned

Ossie (*perplexed*)   England? Are you being serious?

Apha (*loses interest*)   Tell me a joke. Do you know any jokes? I haven't heard a joke in . . . ages. My dad used to tell me jokes.

Ossie (*grabs the straw*)   Your dad? Is this his car?

Apha   Yes. His name's Max. (*His mind seems to drift off and back.*) Did I tell you my dad's name?

Ossie   Yes. Max. Your dad's name is Max.

Apha   Yes.

Ossie   Tell me about Max.

Apha   What do you want to know about him?

Ossie   Anything. What does he do? Where is he? Does he know you're out here tonight in his car?

Apha (*thoughtfully*)   You don't really want to know where he is, do you?

Ossie   Why not?

Apha   I shot him tonight.

Ossie   You what?

Apha   Point-blank. With this –

Apha *casually reaches under his seat and pulls out a pistol. For one horrible moment it looks as if he is going to shoot* **Ossie**. *Then he tosses it into* **Ossie**'s *lap.*

Ossie (*quietly*)   Oh God. Oh God.

Apha   Would you like to see him?

Ossie (*uneasily*)   No.

Apha   He's in the boot.

Ossie   What?! (*To audience.*) Ossie slowly picked up the gun and realised, as he picked it up, that in all his forty years and more, he had never held a gun before.

Apha *stops the car.*

Apha (*getting out*)   Come on.

Ossie   But as Ossie made to open the door, powerful lights suddenly transformed the night into stark, rain-serrated daylight. There were police cars, and helicopters, everywhere.

The performer playing **Apha** *becomes a* **Police Officer** *barking into a megaphone.*

Police Officer (*into megaphone*)   Drop your weapon. You're completely surrounded. Repeat: drop your weapon.

Ossie   Ossie looked at his hand and found he was still holding the weapon. He let it drop to the ground. A while later, he was slammed violently against the car and a pair of handcuffs slapped on to his wrists. He looked around and to his astonishment saw Apha burst into tears.

Apha (*angrily, hysterically*)   He could've killed me! I triggered the alarm ages ago, why did it take you so long to get here?

Police Officer (*into megaphone*)   Drop your weapon. You're completely surrounded. Repeat: drop your weapon.

Ossie (*only slightly panicking*)   What's this, Apha? What's happening here?

Apha   He's in the boot. He put him in the boot. This man killed my dad.

Ossie   Officer –

Ossie   The policeman opened the boot, looked inside briefly, and retched.

Police Officer   What's your name, sir?

Ossie   Jones. Ossie Jones. Officer –

Police Officer (*writes it down*)   'Ossie Jones.' Address?

Ossie   Battersea Park Gardens, London. Officer –

The **Police Officer** *jots this down.*

Police Officer   Occupation?

Ossie   Officer –

Police Officer (*writes it down*)   Occupation: 'Officer.' Right, Ossie Jones. You are under arrest on suspicion of murder.

Ossie (*stunned silence. Then*)   No.

Ossie   It was at this point, as he lay in handcuffs and pressed against the car, that Ossie realised that his dream was in fact a nightmare.

As he speaks, the scene is transformed into a police station.

He had no recollection of the journey to the police station. He tried to wake up from the dream (for he did know it was a dream) by pinching himself and banging his head against everything in sight (including the face of one of the officers between whom he was sandwiched). It was all to no avail. His dream would not let go of him.

I demand a phone. I demand to speak to a lawyer.

The **Detective** *studies him and says nothing. She seems quite amused.*

Ossie   Detective, I *need* to speak to my lawyer.

Detective   All right. What's your lawyer's number?

Ossie   Can I have a phone, please?

Detective (*thrusting a phone at him*)   Go ahead, call your lawyer, Mr Jones.

Ossie (*rifling through his address book*)   This is all a terrible mistake. You'll see, that boy was lying through his teeth. He told me he'd killed his father.

Ossie *dials. And waits.*

Phone Robot   The number you have dialled has not been recognised. Please try again.

Ossie *dials. And waits.*

Phone Robot   The number you have dialled has not been recognised. Please try again.

Ossie *dials another number. And waits.*

Phone Robot   The number you have dialled has not been recognised. Please try again.

Ossie (*trying to look unfazed*)   I must have written down the wrong number. Do you mind if I phone my daughter? She'll know the number. He's her godfather.

The **Dective** *simply stands there looking at him as if he'd just dropped in from another planet.*

Ossie *dials. And waits.*

Phone Robot   The number you have dialled has not been recognised. Please try again.

Ossie   This is absurd.

Ossie   A pronounced panic, low level, from the soles of his feet to the nape of his neck, was beginning to take possession of him. He dialled every single number in his organiser, and several that he knew by heart; he dialled new friends and old acquaintances. He dialled his local pub. He dialled an old enemy who used to be an old friend. He phoned everyone and everywhere, and got the same results.

The **Dective** *seizes the phone from him.*

Detective   Let's start all over again, shall we? Who are you?

Ossie   I've already told you. You've got to believe me.

Detective   Mr Jones – may I call you that – you simply don't exist, Mr Jones. There isn't an Ossie Jones. Not a lawyer, or a plumber, or even a vagrant or a cat. We've checked up every single piece of information you've given us, no records of the driving licence that you gave us, no records of the drink-drive misdemeanour that you claim to have on your record. You have been showering us with a confection of lies, Ossie Jones, and we are beginning to get very, very cross with you. Now, for the last time: who are you and why did you kill Max Wren?

Ossie   Detective – (*in sudden illumination*) I know why those lines are dead, why you think I don't exist. It's because you don't exist! I'm in a dream. I'm dreaming!

The **Detective** *does not even bother to look at him.*

Detective   Ossie Jones's trial was a quick affair. He did not help his case, or endear himself to the judge and the jury by insisting, at every opportunity, that –

Ossie (*hysterically*)   Ha ha, you don't exist! None of you exists!

Detective   Apha was brought in to take the stand.

Ossie   And with a straight face which had even Ossie fooled once or twice Apha described how –

Apha's *speech should be mimed entirely, with emphasis on a stoic demeanour and trauma-driven tearfulness. It should go on for just slightly* longer *than the performer feels comfortable with the silence, at which point* **Ossie** *should interject as follows:*

Ossie   He went on and on and on. Even the public prosecutor yawned once or twice as he listened intently, rearranging his baldness as if it were a wig. . .

Judge   Answer yes or no. Have you reached a verdict in the case of the Crown versus Ossie Jones.

Jury Foreman   Yes.

Judge   How do you find the defendant: guilty or not guilty?

Jury Foreman (*after a pause*)   Guilty.

Ossie *is dragged into a cell.*

Ossie   Ossie was in a haze as he entered his new home to begin his sentence – life without parole. He sat in his cell clawing at his mind, his sagged jaws cupped in the sweat-moistened palms of his hands.

In the prison yard.

Triple-Johni   In the land of dreams, sleep was what happened to you when your mind drifted from wakefulness into a mist of lethargy.

Ossie   His only respite was sleep. When he slept, in this land of dreams, he had no dreams, no nightmares. And sleep was not as he had known it.

Triple-Johni   In the land of dreams you could take a walk, turn on the radio and listen to the weather report, meet up with friends, make love, go to the cinema, play football, or even read the newspaper. You could physically do all these things and more even as you slept.

Ossie   Ossie's choice of things to do was of course circumscribed by the confines of his cell. But he learned fast. A fellow prisoner, a man named –

Triple-Johni   Johni. Triple-Johni.

Ossie   Triple-Johni –

Triple-Johni   Call me Johni.

Ossie   Johni, who also went by the description of Johni-The-Triple-Lifer, was serving three life sentences for homicidal crimes he'd committed during a previous lifetime.

Triple-Johni *nods eagerly.*

Ossie   Johni was thirty when he began the first sentence, and, fortunately for him, died five years later.

Triple-Johni (*whistles with relief*)   Lucky escape.

Ossie   He was born again twenty years after that. Two prison warders were waiting outside the maternity ward when his new mother gave birth to him. He was barely five minutes old when he was handed to them in a nice little pram, which he'd had the forsight to buy during the last few days of his former life.

Triple-Johni   It had been kept for him by one of the prison warders who kept it in the most pristine condition after Johni died and until Johni was born again. The warder cleaned it every year in spring, oiled its wheels and sometimes pushed it to the park and back, just to keep it in shape. As it happened, this same warder was selected by Providence to sire Johni into the world again.

Ossie   Johni was not so lucky during his second life sentence. His plan to die as soon as possible, so he could return, at the earliest opportunity, to serve his third sentence, was what got him into trouble.

Triple-Johni   Death – (*gestures at Ossie, who puts on a death mask*) – knew of his plans –

Death   – and crossed the road to avoid him whenever he saw Triple-Johni approaching.

Triple-Johni   One day, during the morning stroll, he caught sight of Death in the loop of a knot hanging from an improvised rope that another prisoner had just used to commit suicide in a secluded spot behind the prison gym. Death, who looked rather bored and overworked, was dragging the suicide into the world beyond, when Johni arrived at the scene. He ran up to Death and begged him to take him along.

Death *gives him the finger.*

Triple-Johni *pauses, blistering with rage. Then he lunges at* **Death** *and wrestles him to the ground. And proceeds to beat the living daylights out of* **Death**.

Death *manages to wriggle out of* **Triple-Johni**'s *grip and run for dear life.*

Ossie (*takes off the death mask*)   According to those who saw the encounter between Death and Johni-The-Triple-Lifer, and those past whom Death sprinted to get away from Johni, it was as if Death had seen a ghost. Johni, who was a nice guy at heart but a complete psychopath from head-to-toe, bounded after Death.

Triple-Johni   He chased Death up and down the prison threatening to strangle him if Death did not take his life.

Death   Death was traumatised by the incident, and so angry and humiliated, that for twenty years he boycotted the prison and the town in which the prison was situated.

Triple-Johni   During those years not a single person died in that town in the land of dreams, not a single being aged a day older than they were from the day Johni assaulted and chased Death across the prison yard.

Ossie　Those years during which Death inflicted a moratorium on the inmates of the prison and the inhabitants of the town did not prove to be the happiest for them. On the contrary, despondency hung like fog in deepest winter over the prison walls and misery jutted down like icicles from every lamp-post on the streets of the town.

Triple-Johni　This was the reason why: the people found out that in the absence of Death, Life couldn't exist: when Johni chased Death out of the town, he'd inadvertently also chased Life to the city limits and bolted the gates.

Ossie　The outside world convened a conference of philosophers, mathematicians, physicists, metaphysicians, poets, moralists –

Triple-Johni　And taxi drivers – (*by way of explanation*) – who took them there.

Ossie　No minutes of the proceedings were kept; no records of the presentations, or notes of the discussions that took place at the Conference of Life and Death, as that meeting came to be known, exist.

We hear the sudden shrieks of prison alarms.

One day, exactly twenty years later, a great fire broke out in the eastern wing of the prison. No one knew how it started, who started it, or precisely when it started. What was beyond dispute was that by the time the fire ended, several people were dead –

Triple-Johni　(*bitterly*) – and Johni wasn't one of them.

Ossie　Death had returned as dramatically as he had left. The celebrations, all over the land of dreams, went on for weeks. (*Consoles* **Triple-Johni**.) Don't take it so hard, Johni.

Triple-Johni　It's not fair! It's just not fair. (*Makes up his mind.*) I'll tell you what, Ossie.

Ossie   What?

Triple-Johni (*leaving*)   I'm going to go look for that bastard.

Ossie   Who?

Triple-Johni   You know who. I want to know what he thinks he's playing at.

Ossie   Look here, Johni, I really don't think it's a good idea to go beating up Death every time he calls out a name and it isn't yours.

Triple-Johni   Death? Who's talking about Death? I'm talking about the prison governor. This is the second week in a row my cigarette ration's been docked.

He leaves.

Ossie   One morning, fifteen years later, Ossie sat thinking about Johni (who had been dead five years) and dwelling on his daughter Nehushta (whose face haunted his waking moments and his dream-bereft nights: her face was bright and intoxicating like a child's face when it smiles the first time).

There is a knock on his cell door.

A **Warder** *enters.*

Warder   You have a visitor –

Ossie   *A visitor?* (*To audience.*) Ossie followed the warder to the Governor's office.

The **Governor**, *a rather taciturn man, fixes him with a look and then thrusts some forms into Ossie's hands.*

Governor   Sign this, please.

Ossie   What is it?

Governor   Your release papers. You're free.

Ossie *freezes, feeling ill rather than elated. He gropes around and finds a chair.*

Ossie   Where am I supposed to go?

Governor   Sign the forms, please. There's someone outside waiting for you.

Slowly, hand shaking, **Ossie** *signs the forms.*

As Ossie walked across the soccer pitch, which separated the bulk of the prison from the main gates, he watched an ambulance pull in. It stopped beside him. A **Prison Warder** *stepped out of the ambulance, carrying a pram. The pram looked familiar.*

He peeps into the pram and immediately breaks into a grin.

Johni! You're back, Johni! (To **Prison Warder**.) It's Johni, isn't it? Johni-The-Triple-Lifer?

Prison Warder (*glumly*)   It's Triple-Johni all right. Only problem is, the bugger's gone and come back a wee lass.

Ossie (*baffled*)   Johni's now a girl? How come?

Prison Warder   He was born that way.

Ossie   I see.

Pause.

Ossie promised to come back and see little Miss Johni sometime. Outside the prison, there was a car waiting for him. A man stepped out of the car. Ossie's heart stammered when he saw him. It was –

Ossie (*coldly*)   Apha.

Apha   Get in.

Ossie *makes no attempt to get into the car.*

Ossie   What are you doing here, Apha?

Apha   I came to apologise – for all it's worth. And to take you wherever you wish to go.

Ossie   I have no wish to go anywhere with you.

Apha   Please.

Ossie (*truthfully*)   I have nowhere to go.

Apha *takes* **Ossie***'s bag and throws it in the back of the car.*

Apha   I confessed. I told them everything – what really happened. That's why you've been set free.

Ossie   Why did you do it? Why did you frame me?

Apha (*simply*)   Because you were there. I'm sorry.

Ossie (*grudgingly*)   Why are you still free then?

Apha   I'm out on bail. My trial begins next week.

Ossie *is very quiet, his misery in the cup of his hands.*

Apha (*pleads*)   Tell me what you're thinking.

Ossie   I have nowhere to go.

Apha   Why don't you come to my place. Please say yes. It's the least I can do.

Ossie   He said yes. In the land of dreams, objects disappeared the moment you looked away. They travelled backwards and forwards in time and space, to part-time duties in distant planets or brief assignations in parallel universes. They reappeared just as soon as you turned round or opened your eyes to implicate them in your existence.

He lies down to sleep.

The last thing Ossie saw before he fell asleep were Apha's pleading eyes, open wide as if to a fleeting moment of pleasure or a sudden, unexpected terror.

He shuts his eyes, and drifts into sleep.

A radio starts playing. The shipping forecast is on.

Groggily, he emerges from sleep.

He emerged into consciousness. A strange yet familiar smell, disturbing yet comforting, invaded his nostrils and sent self-replicating, self-cancelling signals of joy and sadness to his brain. A radio was in the vicinity. It was tuned to an extraterrestrial station. A strange noise – music – accosted him. His ears stepped tentatively into the room.

He looks tentatively around him.

Ossie opened his eyes and looked around him. There was a woman in the room. She sat in a chair by the bed, reading a book.

(*Weakly, apologetically.*) Excuse me, where am I? (*And then, with a start.*) Nehushta?

The woman looks up and drops the book.

Nehushta Father! Father!

She is screaming and crying at the same time. She runs into his arms.

Ossie/Nehushta Ossie Jones awoke from a coma that had lasted fifteen years.

Ossie Within weeks of emerging from the coma (or, as he liked to call it, his 'subterranean odyssey'), Ossie was given a clean bill of health by the astounded doctors at the west London hospital where, to all appearances, he had vegetated for fifteen years.

Nehushta He was on the front page of every newspaper, and headlined every bulletin on radio and TV. Ossie, his every syllable resonating within relief and gratitude was –

Ossie (*as if to an interviewer*) Simply glad to be back. Thank you. Thank you.

Nehushta Inspired by the awakening, a panel of medical experts, social scientists, politicians and members of the public was invited to a live television debate on the topic of euthanasia. It all ended with everyone accusing everyone else of being, 'politically correct'.

Ossie   'Politically correct?' What does it mean?

Nehushta   It's the great bogeyman from the Pandora's box of the New World Order.

Ossie   Come again?

Nehushta   Pandora's box: 'The first woman brought it with her from Heaven; when she opened it, out of curiosity, all escaped into the world, except Hope.'

Ossie   Ossie nodded patiently, but that was not his question.

Nehushta   His question, which really didn't matter, was –

Ossie   What's the New World Order?

Nehushta *does not respond. He studies her face.*

Ossie   You're very angry with me, aren't you?

Nehushta   No.

Ossie   You're angry with me and your mother.

Nehushta   No.

Ossie   You felt abandoned.

Nehushta (*quietly; nodding*)   Yes.

Ossie (*holding her*)   I'm sorry, Nehushta. I'm really sorry.

They hold each other, comforting each other and crying together.

Ossie   The first thing Ossie did when he was discharged was to visit his late wife Kate's tomb. The visit, to the lush cemetery in the direction of Dover, took place on one of those bright summer days when scantily clad natives of London, vying with tourists wearing baseball caps and sombreros, unleash themselves on the outdoors with the singular and inexorable ferocity of an act of nature.

Nehushta   It's quite busy in here today, isn't it?

Ossie   At the cemetery they made their way through a
throng of visitors, and across a serrated mass of headstones,
to Kate's resting place. At each gravestone they went by,
they saw families laden with hampers packed with food,
crockery and cutlery, and sitting on mats spread out on the
grass among the yew trees. One or two shouted out
greetings to them.

Nehushta (*waves*)   Nice people, aren't they?

Ossie   As they went further into the graveyard, these
picnics of the dead became rare, and soon there were none.
A sombre and elegiac mood, crystallising into an inarticulate
celebration of silence, came over them.

They walk on, quietly, in total silence.

Nehushta   Soon they arrived at their destination, a
simple headstone inscribed with Kate's name. They lay
down the flowers they had brought and sat down to talk to
Kate. They tossed a coin to decide who should go first.

Ossie   She won.

Nehushta   She made herself comfortable and proceeded
to tell her mother that she had dumped Russell.

Ossie   Russell?

Nehushta   My boyfriend.

*She barely pauses as she pours a bottle of wine into three glasses, one of
which she places beside the flowers.*

Cheers, Mum. Welcome back, Dad.

Ossie   To Kate – you're alive because every time we
breathe, you breathe in us. And to you, our daughter, our
beautiful daughter – who looks just like you, Kate – and to
us all.

They clink their glasses against Kate's.

(*Oh-so-casually*) How long were you with Russell?

Nehushta (*laughing*)   Six months. Don't worry, Mum knew all about it.

Ossie   And why are you no longer together?

Nehushta   Because we split up, Dad. Shut up, will you. I'm trying to have a conversation with Mum.

(*To audience.*) And she went on to tell Kate how, actually only a week before Ossie rose from the dead –

(*To Kate.*) Oops, Mum! I mean, from his coma, I decided I'd had it with Russell's self-obsessiveness.

Ossie   Ossie listened, feeling guilty, as if he were eavesdropping on an intimate conversation between two people he no longer knew as well as he used to . . .

Nehushta (*to Kate*)   Did I tell you, Mum, that his idea of foreplay was ten minutes of begging . . . !

Ossie   The thirteen-year-old girl he had left behind had become the altogether grown-up woman sitting beside him on the grass. As she went on talking to her mother, another penny dropped, and he felt an immense relief, a deep gratitude to her: he realised that this prattle with her mother about her private life was also, indirectly, a conversation with him. Sitting there in the sun, with his daughter talking to him through her mother, he felt sad, and happy in his sadness.

Nehushta   Oh, by the way, Mum, we're going on holiday.

Ossie (*surprised*)   Who are 'we'? And where are they going?

Nehushta   Me and my friend. His name is . . . on the ticket.

She pulls out two tickets from her bag and gives them to him.

Nehushta (*as he studies the tickets*)   I took out my savings.

Ossie   You did what? We've got some serious talking to do, young lady.

Nehushta   I was planning on going anyway – with Russell.

Ossie   Would you have paid for him as well?

Nehushta   No. But he hadn't been lying in a coma for fifteen years. And he sure isn't my father. Listen, Dad, I want you to come along.

Ossie   When did you make this incontestable decision to co-opt me into this?

Nehushta   Really, Dad, you don't have to if you don't want to.

Ossie (*after a short silence*)   Try stopping me.

Nehushta *starts hooting with delight.*

Ossie   On one condition, though.

Nehushta   What?

Ossie   I pay for everything else: food, hotels –

Nehushta   Deal.

The scene transforms into a street in Brixton.

A soapbox evangelist, wearing a sandwich-board which states: 'Twelve Tribes of Israel', is in full flow.

Twelve Tribalist 1 (*with a North American accent*)   What was that you said?

Twelve Tribalist 2   *Much* every way.

Twelve Tribalist 1   Say that again.

Twelve Tribalist 2   Much *every* way.

Twelve Tribalist 1   Much every way. Because the Israelites the Jews, when we get the earth, when the so-called black Americans and Negroes, the West Indians, the

Haitians, the Dominicans, the Puerto Ricans, the North
American Indians, the Cubans, the Ecuadorians, all the way
down to the Mexicans, when we get the earth back again,
we gon' control everythin'. OK. The Kingdom of Heaven is
only for one people. Only for one people – and that's it. We
been taught the Kingdom of Heaven's for everybody – but
it don't say that in the Bible. Read.

Twelve Tribalist 2 (*reads*)   'Unto them were committed
the oracles of God.'

Twelve Tribalist 1   Because –

Twelve Tribalist 2   'Unto them was given the oracles of
the Most High'.

Twelve Tribalist 1   The Oracles of God are the laws,
statutes and commandments. And that was only given to
one people. OK. First of all, Christ didn't come for all
nations, he came for one people. He was only the saviour of
one nation. Accordin' to the Bible. We gon' read that for
you –

A tiny woman, who shall go by the name of the **Ecstatic**, *raises her
hand.*

Ecstatic   Can I ask a question, please?

Twelve Tribalist 1   Er –

Ecstatic   Do you know most of these people who sayin'
they is pastor and preach in the church, they're the more
Devil?

Twelve Tribalist 1   Yeah.

Ecstatic (*ecstatically*)   You know dat!

Twelve Tribalist 1 (*trying to move on*)   Yes. OK –

Ecstatic   I went to church last Sunday. And if I'm sick,
they're supposed to 'eal me and dem wan' trow me out.

Twelve Tribalist 1   That's right. The Bible says –

Ecstatic (*indignantly*)   Dem are no God.

Ossie *and* **Nehushta** *move on.*

Nehushta   Seriously, Dad, what you told Mum this afternoon – all that stuff about 'the land of dreams' . . .

Ossie   Every word, every last punctuation mark.

Nehushta   Jeeze. Why didn't you tell the doctors when you woke up?

Ossie   It did cross my mind, but it seemed so incredulous – even to me – I thought it was better not to. I didn't want them starting to worry about the state of my mind.

Nehushta   Have you been . . . back there since you . . . returned?

Ossie   Back where?

Nehushta   You know . . . the land of dreams . . .

Ossie   Don't be ridiculous.

Nehushta   I'm being totally serious. Doesn't it bother you that it could happen again?

Ossie (*shaking his head, emphatically*)   No, I don't think it would.

(*To audience.*)

And then, for his sins, she dragged him along to see a play in a tiny theatre up above a pub. The play was something called – (*Consults the programme.*)

Nehushta (*as* **Ossie** *reaches for his reading glasses.*)   *Cool Killers.*

Ossie (*puts on his glasses*)   Yes. (*Wryly.*) 'Cool Killers.'

Ossie   *Cool Killers* was the story of two gentlemen named Mister Noir and – (*Consults the programme again.*)

Ossie   The two men were trapped in what looked like . . . an elephant. (*To audience.*) She designed the set.

(*To* **Nehushta**.) Why are they trapped in an elephant? Is it a metaphor for the human condition?

Nehushta (*gives him a look*) It's a car, Dad.

Ossie   Ah, I see. The elephant is a metaphor for a car.

Nehushta (*gives him another look*)   No, Dad, it's not an elephant. It's . . . a car.

Ossie   A car that looks like an elephant.

Nehushta   They are sitting in a car somewhere in Peckham. They are waiting to make a hit.

Ossie   A *what?*

Nehushta   Just watch, Dad. OK?

Ossie   Mister Noir chewed gum loudly and scratched and, or, rearranged his testicles every few seconds. Mister Blanc had more or less the same habits, although he did not scratch his testicles nearly so often. They were dressed in black – (*as they become* **Mister Noir** *and* **Mister Blanc**) – dark suits, dark shoes and dark glasses. These, combined with the dark, shimmering guns lying on the dashboard, endowed the two men with a mildly sinister presence.

Mister Noir *checks his watch. Then he looks into the far distance. He scratches his scrotum and takes a long drag at his cigarette.*

Mister Noir   He always gets up at six on the dot, without fail.

Mister Blanc   Supposing today he doesn't?

Mister Noir   Then we go in there and ask him why not. Sit back, all right? Relax. I've done this . . . so long as things go strictly according to plan, and you're alert when you have to improvise, it's a piece of cake.

Mister Blanc   What's his story?

Mister Noir   What's his story? I don't know what his story is. I don't know that he even has a story.

Pause.

Even if he did have a story do I wanna hear it? No, thank you, I don't wanna hear it. Do you wanna hear it? No. You don't wanna hear it, believe me, you do not wanna hear that man's story. Why not? Because if you did then what the fuck are you doing in this army?

Ossie Ah, they are soldiers.

Nehushta No, they're not. Shush.

Ossie Yes they are.

Mister Noir What the fuck are you doing in any army, for that matter?

Ossie (*nudges* **Nehushta**) He said it again. They are soldiers.

She ignores him.

Mister Noir (*now on a roll*) What I'm saying is, and this is a *for instance*, if you're a soldier and you're sent to war, you're sent there to hurt the enemy, to subvert, to kill him, to eliminate him, to make dust of his dreams. Your bullet is the full stop at the end of his life, *period*. That's what you're sent there to do. Simple arithmetic: subtract him from himself.

A light comes on in the far distance.

See that light, six on the dot. That's what I call being reliable. D'you know Woody Allen?

Mister Blanc Are you kidding? I went to school with him.

Mister Noir Go on, brag about it. In one of his films Woody says –

Mister Blanc Woody, ay?

Mister Noir He says, 'Crime pays. The hours are good, you travel a lot.' Guess what: he's right. Did you see *Crimes and Misdemeanours*?

Mister Blanc   Yeah, my favourite actor, the dog. Are you mad, or what? We're on the verge of sending someone to that great place in the sky and all you can find to talk about is Woody –

Mister Noir   'The great place in the sky.' And you say *I'm* being flippant. You don't like Woody Allen, is that what you're saying?

Mister Blanc (*heatedly*)   That's not what I said.

Mister Noir   I'll tell you why you don't like him –

Mister Blanc   I never said I didn't like him!

Mister Noir   – It's because you're scared of emotions –

Mister Blanc   Fuck you.

Mister Noir   It's true. You're afraid of expressing yourself.

Mister Blanc   I can't believe I'm hearing this.

Mister Noir   That's how come you never scored with Emma.

Mister Blanc   Some relationships go beyond the mere physical, you know. There's something called a spiritual dimension.

Mister Noir   Yeah? What goes on there: virtual copulation?

Mister Blanc   You know, I feel sorry for guys like you.

Mister Noir   Guys like me! Who was the wise guy who kept sending flowers to Emma for a whole year and didn't even get to see her underwear – in the laundry – let alone –

Mister Blanc   Hey, let's set the records straight once and for all: I never sent her any flowers. I never sent her a single flower.

Mister Noir (*looks shocked, incredulous*)   You didn't?

Mister Blanc   I fucking didn't.

Mister Noir   Not even on Val's Day?

Mister Blanc   Val's Day my ass.

Mister Noir   You see what I'm saying? It comes back to: you're afraid of your emotions, the lover in you. That's why you don't like Woody Allen.

Mister Blanc   If shagging your own daughter –

Mister Noir   She wasn't his daughter.

Mister Blanc   If shagging your own daughter is what you call being romantic, then, yes, I'm not romantic.

Mister Noir   She wasn't his daughter and, anyway, don't use words like that: shagging. I hate it when people use words like that. What happened to good old 'love-making' . . . making love? Shagging. Shafted. 'They copulated.' Fuckingchrist, what are 'they': train carriages? 'He had carnal knowledge of her.' Where? On a butcher's slab? I mean, fuckingchrist, I'd rather you said, 'They fucked.' At least that's unpretentious, and it captures something of the essence of – (*Breaks into a grin.*) I'm a New Man.

Mister Blanc   Oh, really? Haven't you heard he never existed?

Mister Noir   Bollocks. Take it from me, it's the only way to get laid these days. And look, it's all right to do that Woody Allen-is-a-prick thing. Just don't lay it on too thick.

Mister Blanc   For the hundredth time, I'm telling you, Woody bloody Allen – (*Stops suddenly. He's seen something.*)

That's him. He's coming out.

Mister Noir *looks. Slowly,* **Mister Noir** *picks up his gun, does a few things to it, and then takes aim. As he is about to pull the trigger, there is a blackout.*

In the darkness that ensues:

Nehushta (*after a pause*) Dad?

Ossie Yes?

Nehushta What do you think?

Ossie (*after a thoughtful pause*) I think I need a strong drink.

When the lights rise again, **Ossie** *and* **Nehushta** *are downstairs in the pub.* **Ossie** *watches as* **Nehushta** *kisses and is kissed, hugs and is hugged by a seemingly endlessly stream of people. At long last she comes and joins him.*

Nehushta Now, Dad, tell me, how did the play strike you?

But before he can respond she spots two people passing them.

(*Kiss, kiss, hug, hug*) Hello, darling! Hello, sweetheart! This is my dad. He absolutely loved it. Didn't you, Dad? Dad, meet Ron. Ron wrote the play. Joe directed it.

Ossie *takes a huge gulp of his beer and shakes their hands.*

Ossie (*after* **Ron** *and* **Joe** *have gone*) Why do they both look like they been kicked by a mule?

Nehushta They have that effect on each other whenever they're forced to breathe the same air. (*Brightly.*) So, how did it strike you?

Ossie How did it strike me?

Nehushta Honestly.

Ossie Honestly and frankly?

Nehushta Frankly and honestly.

Ossie Well, if you mean, did I like it, the answer is, yes I did and no I didn't.

Nehushta How do you mean and how don't you?

Ossie (*grins*) I liked the way it said what it was saying, but I didn't think it was saying anything or that it had anything to say. But I believe in freedom of speech. I believe that everybody who has absolutely nothing to say has the God-given, inalienable right to say it. I think that in writing this play, the writer was merely exercising that fundamental human right and should neither be applauded nor chastised for doing so. On the other hand, I think it's quite brazen of him to require me to pay him to do so.

Nehushta   You came in on a comp, Dad. And it's not really as bad as it seems.

Ossie   That's what the Invisible Man said. 'I'm not as bad as I look.' Seriously though – (*Smoothly.*) The best thing this production has going for it is, I think, the stage design. It achieves a certain symmetry, a coherence of vision that is lacking in the rest of the show.

Nehushta   Flattery, and a travelcard, will get you anywhere, Dad. But I still disagree with you. I do think the playwright has something to say, and that it does come across in the play.

Ossie   And what's this thing that he has to say?

Nehushta   It's not so much a message as a mood that he's trying to put across. I think he's trying to capture the *Zeitgeist*. It's all about art imitating art imitating art.

Ossie   Aha. Now I understand, that's why the characters all sound like characters trying to sound like characters trying to sound like characters.

Nehushta   Since you've been away, Dad, not only has the world got meta and meta, every post- has been postponed.

Ossie   And how is the postal system coping with the deluge?

Nehushta   Admirably well, all things considered – (*Then, deliberately stepping on his foot.*) Oops, sorry, Dad.

Ossie   What I'm saying – and I will not be intimidated, lady – is this: what happened to the chronicling of recognisable, three-dimensional, plain simple folk? What

happened to Joe-and-Jane-on-the-street? What happened to
art imitating and celebrating, or interrogating and re-
imagining reality?

Nehushta   Hit men *do* exist, Dad.

Ossie   Yes, but how many does your playwright know?

Nehushta   All right, Dad, I give up.

Ossie   Good. Shall we go home now?

Nehushta   In a moment. But first, I'd like you to meet the
cast. (*Gestures.*) They're seated right over there.

She makes to go.

Ossie *does not move.*

Nehushta (*pleads*)   Come on, Dad. They're friends of
mine.

Ossie (*imitates her*)   'Come on, Dad. They're friends of
mine.' Tell me, what should I say if they asked me what I
thought of the play?

Nehushta   The truth, Dad, tell them the truth.

Ossie   The truth? The unvarnished truth?

Nehushta   The truth – varnished, unvarnished, in
whatever shape or form. As long as it's the truth.

Pause.

But under no circumstance must you tell them you didn't
like their performance.

Ossie   You are asking me to lie?

Nehushta   I'm asking you to show some sensitivity.

Ossie   But I didn't like their performance.

Nehushta   Then don't mention their performance.

Ossie   I can't just *not* mention their performance.

Nehushta   Get in there first. Ask them what they thought of their performance.

Ossie   And if they thought they were brilliant?

Nehushta   Tell them you absolutely adored their suits.

Ossie   I positively hated their suits.

Nehushta   It's only a matter of verbs, Dad, you're welcome to borrow mine.

Ossie   You can keep your verbs. I'm perfectly happy with mine.

Nehushta   Come on, Dad! Tell them . . . I don't know . . . tell them certain aspects of the play reminded you of a play by Harold Pinter. Then talk about Harold Pinter.

Ossie   I don't know much about Harold Pinter.

Nehushta   Use your nous, Dad.

Ossie   'Meta' and now 'nous'! Where do you get these strange words from?

Nehushta   Come on now. It should be relatively painless. You are a lawyer after all.

Ossie   That is a very wicked thing to say.

(*To audience.*) It turned out that the thespians were having a party that night.

(*Extends his hand to* **Nehushta**)

Shall we?

Ossie *and* **Nehushta** *dance together to Fats Waller's 'You're Not the Only Oyster in the Stew'.*

Later, on the night-bus.

The Man   The most important part of the process, when the bottles are being aged –

Nehushta   Well-dressed man in the seat behind them –

Ossie   On the night bus as they headed back home –

The Man   The most important part of the process, is that they must be turned ninety degrees every day. They've got these guys who are professional bottle-turners –

Ossie   He patiently explained to the woman in front of him –

Nehushta (*points to herself*) ˙ Nehushta.

Ossie   Who, it seemed, had invited the man's attention by virtue of the fact that there was no one else on the bus –

Nehushta   And because the man she was travelling with –

Ossie (*points to himself*)   Ossie.

Nehushta   Was snoring loudly beside her.

Ossie *snores.*

The Man   The bottle-turners spend three years in apprenticeship, learning the art of turning up to a hundred bottles a minute. As you can guess, this is hard on the wrists so the average span of a bottle-turner's career is seven years.

Pauses, as if to let it sink in.

Have you ever wondered why there's that conical indentation in the bottom of champagne bottles?

Nehushta (*subtly trying to nudge* **Ossie** *to wake up*)   She shakes her head and then almost in the same moment nods vigorously.

The Man   Well, Dom Perignon, the monsieur who started it all, realized that carbonation builds up great pressure inside a bottle. When one bottle in the rack bursts, it destroys many bottles around it. So he redesigned the bottle, forcing the pressure to escape along the length of the bottle, rather than equally out, so it does not tend to break other bottles in the rack.

Nehushta (*Silent. Finally.*)   Why are you telling me all this?

Ossie   At that moment, the bus pulled to stop and a
deluge of night-crawlers and early-risers, including a tall,
middle-aged Rastaman talking at the top of his voice to a
younger man, who nodded off in his seat as soon as he sat
down, got on the night bus.

The Rastaman   But now I met dis woman, Elizabeth de
Cathalic, who tell me her life story, an' it sorta lift sense
away from nonsence. Dere is a book who say dere was a
queen down here by name Mary Elizabeth de Cathalic,
true, which they actually killed fe true. No doubt about it,
dis woman I have met who came down here, Mary
Elizabeth de Cathalic, she a ghost all right. Anyway when I
was sorta lookin' back to everyting, everyting sorta give me
a little bit of understandin' about the Blessed Virgin Mary.
Fe true, really they murder her. Now dis woman, she have
dis man wid her, right. He's a brown man like, who she
have as her son – Jesus Christ. Who reveal himself to me as
Selassie I. Dis match up wid what Rastaman been
preachin', dat is a Rastaman, Jesus Christ, who actually
reveal himself as Selassie I. I could never understand why
Rastaman been sayin' Jesus Christ was Sellasie I, but when I
met dis woman, dis white woman, Elizabeth de Cathalic,
and dis brown man, her son, sen I could see sense outta
nonsense . . .

Ossie   Sometime later, Ossie felt a nudge in his rib. It was
Nehushta waking him up.

Nehushta   This is us.

Ossie   Someone coughed, another person sneezed, and
somebody shouted for Megan to get with it. He opened his
eyes and was blinded briefly by a shimmering daguerreotype
of bleached-out feet shuffling towards the exit, which, in the
astigmatic provenance of his eyes, took on the shape of a
long and narrowing hole that led in a blurred trail across his
nose and into infinity and beyond.

He sees the bottle **Nehushta** *is holding.*

(*Stirring*) What's that?

Nehushta   Champagne. This guy on the bus said I could have it.

Ossie (*puzzled*)   Why?

Nehushta   He said in case I didn't like beer.

Ossie   Brixton, when they got back there in the early hours, was as busy, almost, as they'd left it the evening before; the same dream-vendors –

Ossie/Nehushta   The same dream-seekers.

Ossie/Nehushta   The same shape-shifters.

Ossie/Nehushta   The same conjurer-clowns.

Ossie/Nehushta   The same moonstruck-magicians.

Ossie/Nehushta   The same deities.

Ossie/Nehushta   The same demons.

Nehushta   The same day.

Ossie   And the same night; a night illuminated, not by stars, but by a luminous constellation of hopes. Up the hill, near Nehushta's flat, they passed a man walking his dog. They met another man pushing a synthesiser in a baby buggy. As Ossie walked hand in hand with his daughter, he felt a glow in his heart. Dreams were made of nights like this.

They are back in **Nehushta**'s *flat.* **Ossie** *collapses in exhaustion.*

Ossie (*holding* **Nehushta**)   I had a dream tonight, on the bus, on our way back home. I must have nodded off for a few seconds. During those few seconds, as I sank into darkness, a great fear gripped me and, without a thought, I called out – in my mind – I called out your name. And at that moment, your face seemed to emerge, haunting and dimly seen, as from the fading brilliance of a great sunset. And it banished my fear. Fats Waller, the great jazz man,

I think it was who used to say, 'Kill me while I'm happy!'
I felt so happy tonight, I could have died.

Nehushta (*happy, tired*)   Good night, Dad.

Ossie   Good night, Nehushta.

She leaves.

As he lay in bed that night, Ossie thought of the slouching
shadows of lonesome giants and the radiance of a shared
moment, the syncopated silence of selective amnesia and the
resonating infinitude of a done deed, the ticking of time and
the hypothesis of immortality, the threat of rain and the
beauty of a green landscape, the falling out of teeth and the
serenity of a toothless smile, the numbing shock of a sudden
disappointment and the lingering scream into which an
orgasm erupts. (*Yawns.*) Just before he drifted into sleep,
Ossie thought of Kate, who died giving birth to Nehushta.
He wished Kate was here with them. But he couldn't have
everything. He had Nehushta. They had each other. And
that was more than enough. Happiness, he decided, was a
journey out of a nightmare and into a dream. He felt very,
very happy.

He crawls into bed and immediately falls asleep.

A moment later, **Nehushta** *enters.*
She switches off the bedside lamp.
She leaves.

Lights fade to black.

Happy Birthday, Mister Deka D

Happy Birthday, Mister Deka D was first performed at the Traverse Theatre Edinburgh on 10 August 1999. It received its London premiere at the Lyric Theatre Hammersmith on 8 November 1999. The cast was as follows:

Lika	Hayley Carmichael
Mister Deka D	Richard Clews
Trisk	Paul Hunter

Directed by John Wright
Designed by Naomi Wilkinson

A spotlight captures **Mister Deka D***'s inscrutably grinning face. His head, glistening, is bereft of hair. He is still, statuesque.*

Lights rise to reveal that he is seated at the lone table in a dank, poorly lit pub with grimy walls and cigarette-smoke-smudged blinds.

Facing **Mister Deka D**, *on the other side of the table – and separated from him by two empty chairs – is* **Lika***, reading a newspaper – or rather, short-sightedly squinting at it and silently mouthing the words to herself.*

The bar is dust-laden and enveloped in cobwebs.

Two strings, strewn with 'Happy Birthday' cards lined like laundry spread out to dry, stretch from one end of the ceiling to the other, intersecting midpoint to form a slightly skewered X.

The doorbell rings.

Mister Deka D *remains immobile. His moronic grin is not one bit ruffled.*

Lika *lets it ring several times before she looks up from the newspaper.*

Lika (*shouts*)   It's open. (*Louder.*) The door's open.

Pause.

Enter **Trisk***, barefooted. Slung across his shoulders is a pair of shoes, tied together at the laces.*

Pause as **Lika** *looks at him, vaguely and slightly suspiciously at first. Then, recognising him, she calls out to him.*

A monumentally loud drill, coming from the flat upstairs, suddenly comes on, drowning the conversation.

Lika *and* **Trisk** *continue talking. We watch their mouths move but cannot hear a single word of the spirited exchange.*

Not once during this scenario does either of them even look up to the ceiling or visually acknowledge the source of the noise.

Mister Deka D*'s moronic grin is not one bit ruffled.*

Trisk *and* **Lika** *embrace, or rather, he embraces her.*

The noise stops as suddenly as it began. The silence catches **Lika** *and* **Trisk** *in mid-conversation.*

Trisk   It's well past closing time. Were you expecting someone?

Lika   No.

Trisk   Why's the door still open?

Lika   The door is always open.

Trisk   It was shut yesterday when I went by.

Lika   Sometimes it's always shut.

Trisk   Did you know I was coming?

Lika   No.

Trisk   Did you know I was in town?

Lika   No.

Trisk   I've been back for ages. Did you know that?

Lika   No.

Trisk   Are you serious?

Lika   No.

Trisk   So you knew?

Lika   No.

Trisk   Did you know I was still alive?

Lika   No.

Trisk   Did you think I was dead?

Lika   No.

Trisk   What did you think?

Lika   I didn't.

Trisk   Did you care one way or the other?

Lika   No.

Pause.

Trisk   Do you want me to stay?

Lika   No.

Trisk   Do you want me to leave?

Lika   No.

Trisk   What do you want me to do?

Lika   Put on your shoes.

Trisk   Of course. I was in such a hurry to get dressed, I forgot to put on my shoes.

He begins to put on his shoes.

Lika   Why were you in a hurry to get dressed?

Trisk   I'm always in a hurry to get dressed. I think it comes from being born naked. (*Examines his shoes.*) I always forget to wear them, but I never forget to take them with me wherever I'm going.

Lika   And why's that?

Trisk   My mother used to say to me – bless her – she used to say to me, 'Always take your shoes with you, son, you never know where you might find a road.'

Lika   She called you 'son'?

Trisk   She seemed to think she was my mother. (*With genuine pleasure.*) It's so nice to see you again, Lika. It's been such a long time –

Lika (*yawning*)   Yes.

Trisk   Since.

Lika   Yes.

Trisk   Since?

Lika   Yes?

Trisk *sneezes.*

Trisk (*apologetically*)   I think I may have caught a bug.

Pause.

Lika *goes to the bar and fetches a bottle and two glasses. She blows into the glasses and a cloud of dust rises in the air.*

Lika (*pouring*)   Nice coat.

She hands him a glass. They clink glasses and both knock back the drinks at the same time.

(*Pouring another round.*)   I had one myself. Gave it to charity.

Trisk   You gave a cold to charity?

Lika   A coat. Just like yours.

Trisk   You've lost me there.

Lika (*distractedly*)   Where?

Trisk *searches in vain for something in his pockets.*

Trisk   On the tube. I must have left it on the tube. I (*sneezes*), you see, on the tube. My whole body shook. That's when it must have fallen out. Some happy bastard's now lighting a cigarette with my box of matches. (*Pensively.*) Where's the justice in that?

Lika (*pointing to an object on the table*)   There.

Trisk   What? (*He reaches behind his ear and pulls out a cigarette.*) Do you have a light?

Lika *ignores him and returns to her newspaper.*

Trisk *picks up an object beside a cake. It's a cigarette lighter. He lights the cigarette. He drops the lighter back on the table, and pensively smokes in silence.*

He goes and sits beside **Mister Deka D** *but doesn't appear to notice him. He focuses instead on the one empty chair at the table.*

Trisk (*ominously*)   She's not here.

Lika (*without looking up*)   She's not.

Trisk (*angrily*)   She's not here.

Lika (*looking up, as if surprised*)   She's not?

Trisk (*pensively*)   Well, is she? Is she?

Lika (*gesturing at the empty chair*)   Oh, you mean *her*?

Trisk   Oh, did she? Did she say she was going to be late?

Lika   She phoned.

Trisk   I know she phoned, you just said so a moment ago. (*Irritably.*) I'm not deaf, you know. There's no need to repeat yourself.

Lika   I'm not repeating myself.

Trisk   You are.

Lika   No, I'm not.

Trisk   Yes, you are.

Lika (*shouting*)   No, I'm not. (*Pause.*) What did she say when she phoned?

Pause.

Trisk   She said she was going to be late.

Lika   Did she?

Trisk   I don't know, Lika, you're the one who spoke to her.

Lika   I said she phoned, I didn't say I spoke to her.

Trisk   What, she left a message?

Lika   I said she phoned, I didn't say she left a message.

Trisk   What did she do when she phoned?

Lika   She spoke.

Trisk   Naturally. That's good. It's good to speak when you make a phone call.

Lika   She spoke but it was a bad line.

Trisk   The line was bad?

Lika   Yes. She could hear herself. I could hear myself. But we couldn't hear each other.

Trisk   How do you know she could hear herself?

Lika   I said the line was bad, I didn't say she was deaf.

Trisk   How do you know it was her?

Lika   Did you phone?

Trisk   No.

Lika   Just as I thought. I knew if it wasn't you, it had to be her.

Trisk   And how did you know it wasn't me?

Lika   It wasn't, was it?

Trisk   I just told you, I didn't phone.

Lika   *She* phoned. She was the one.

Trisk (*gives in*)   She's always late.

Lika   Is she? I've never known her to be late, have you?

Trisk   Not until now.

Lika   Then why do you say she's always late?

Trisk   Every next second she's late is another instance of being late.

Lika   Really.

Trisk   When she shows up she'd have been late so many times I wouldn't bother to show up if I were in her shoes.

Pause.

Lika   Only enough for one person and I was just about to help myself to it.

Trisk   *What?*

Lika   You said you could do with some coffee.

Trisk   No, I didn't, but that's all right. I was just about to ask you anyway.

Lika   Go ahead, ask.

Trisk   I could do with a coffee. Can I have some coffee?

Lika *pulls out a flask by her side and pours into a mug.*

Lika   I just told you, only enough for me. Besides, I've run out of sugar.

Trisk, *with a flourish, produces two lumps of sugar.*

Lika   All right then, you're welcome to half of the coffee.

Trisk   Are you sure? Is that spoken from the heart?

Lika   Yes.

Trisk   You go first. Drink the first half, I'll have the rest.

Lika   Can I have some of your sugar?

Trisk   Out of the question.

Lika   Why?

Trisk   I've only got enough for one.

Lika   Does that mean no?

Trisk   You know I've got a sweet tooth, Lika.

Lika   *I'm* sharing *my* coffee with you, Trisk.

Pause.

Trisk *will not budge.*

Lika (*peeved*)   You go first.

Trisk   Are you sure? Spoken from the heart?

Lika   Yes.

Trisk (*shrugs*)   All right.

He makes as if to throw the two lumps of sugar in the coffee but at the last moment, flings one into his mouth and washes it down his throat with a gurgled gulp of coffee.

Lika   Wait, wait. I've changed my mind, I'll go first.

She takes the mug from him, gets up and begins to go out.

Trisk   Where are you off to?

Lika   To the kitchen.

Trisk   Why?

Lika   To fetch some salt.

Trisk   Why?

Lika   I've decided to drink mine with salt.

As **Trisk** *makes to respond, the phone rings and they both jump.*
Lika *drops the jug and spills the coffee on the floor.*

Lika (*running to the phone*)   Must be her. (*She gets the phone.*)
'Hello, is that you? Hello? . . . Hello, speak up . . . the line's
bad, I can't hear you . . . Hello, is that you? Is that? Is that?'
(*She gives up, puts down the phone.*)

Trisk   Was it her?

Lika   Yes.

Trisk   And the line was bad *again*?

Lika   What do you mean *again*?

Trisk   You said she called earlier.

Lika   I was referring to this call.

Pause.

Trisk   How could you have been referring to a call that
hadn't been made?

Lika (*patiently*)   But it *has* been made, Trisk.

Trisk   It hadn't when you referred to it.

Lika   It now has. And that's all that matters. (*Pause.*) No, I'm not.

Trisk   Are you married?

Lika   None.

Trisk   Children? (*Pause.*) See? You answer my questions even before I ask them. (*Pause.*) Half eleven.

Lika   What time is it?

Trisk   I just told you. (*Pause, then panic.*) What are you doing to me, Lika? What –

A loud drill, coming from the flat upstairs, completely drowns his voice.

Lika *and* **Trisk** *hold a long, frenzied conversation that is totally drowned by the thundering drill. We watch their mouths move but cannot hear a single word of the spirited exchange.*

Not once during this scenario does either of them even look up to the ceiling or visually acknowledge the source of the noise.

Deka*'s moronic grin is not one bit ruffled.*

The noise stops as suddenly as it began. The silence catches **Lika** *and* **Trisk** *in mid-conversation.*

Trisk   . . . (ne)ver again?

Lika   Never.

Trisk   Oh, Lika, I'm sorry to hear that. Does it still hurt?

Lika   Oh yes, I did.

Trisk   Did you love him?

Lika   Oh yes, it does. (*Pause.*) That doesn't sound quite right.

Trisk   No, it doesn't.

Lika   Ask me those questions again.

Trisk   Are you sure? Is that spoken from the heart?

Lika   Yes (yes).

Trisk   All right. Tell me when you're ready.

Lika   Go ahead.

Trisk   Right. Does it still hurt?

Lika   Oh yes, it does.

Trisk   Did you love him?

Lika   Oh yes, I did.

Pause.

Trisk   Much better.

Pause.

Lika   That wasn't the end of it though.

Trisk   It wasn't?

Lika   No, it wasn't. I heard from him a year later.

Trisk   He wrote you a letter?

Lika   No.

Trisk   He came running back?

Lika   No.

Trisk   What did he do?

Lika (*portentously*)   He phoned.

Trisk   Is that true? Is that really what he did?

Lika   Yes.

Trisk   Spoken from the heart?

Lika   No.

Trisk   Did he or didn't he phone?

Lika   He phoned. I just told you he phoned.

Trisk   He phoned. And it wasn't a bad line?

Lika   He phoned. It wasn't a bad line.

Trisk   He could hear himself.

Lika   And I could hear myself.

Trisk   And you could hear each other?

Lika (*nods*)   And we could hear each other.

Trisk   Now there's what I call a miracle. A phone that talks back.

Lika   And you know the first thing he said?

Trisk (*loses interest*)   I've just become a father, Lika.

Lika (*pauses, surprised*)   Yes, that's what he said.

Trisk   No, Lika, I mean *I* . . .

Lika   I said, 'Congratulations, is it a boy or a girl?'

Trisk   Lika.

Lika   'Yes,' he said, something stunned, 'but how did you know?'

Trisk   *I* have become a father, Lika.

Lika   I didn't realise he was such a moron.

Trisk   A moron?

Lika   Yes.

Trisk   A fool.

Lika   Yes.

Trisk   A moron.

Lika   Yes.

Trisk   A fool?

Lika   Yes.

Trisk   Take it from me, Lika, if you haven't been out with a moron, you haven't.

Lika   I know.

Trisk (*with conviction*)   You simply haven't.

Lika   I know, Trisk.

Trisk   That's what my mother used to say. (*Pause.*) How did you *know* it was a boy or a girl?

Lika (*equally serious, with a tinge of pride*)   I guessed.

Lika *returns to her newspaper.*

Trisk *fidgets for a while.*

Mister Deka D *stirs from his moronic stupor. He gets up and, without the slightest change in his expression, heads straight to a door marked 'Ladies'.*

Trisk *notices* **Mister Deka D** *for the first time. He stares as* **Mister Deka D** *emerges from the 'Ladies' and heads into an adjacent door marked 'Gentlemen'.*

There is a long silence.

Trisk   Who is that?

Lika   Who?

The sound of a toilet being flushed resounds from the Gents.

Trisk (*nods at the Gents*)   Him in there.

Lika (*yawns*)   Oh, Mister Deka D. He used to be a regular here, when Number 1, 2, 3, 4, 5 was still a pub.

Trisk   When it *was* still a pub?

Lika   We're no longer trading.

Trisk   Why not?

Lika   We lost our licence.

Trisk   How come?

Lika   Because.

Pause.

Trisk   I see. Why does he still come here then?

Lika (*shrugs*)   I haven't asked him.

Trisk   Why haven't you asked him?

Lika   He owns the place.

Mister Deka D *emerges from the Gents, expression resolutely unchanged, and resumes his position at the table.*

Pause.

Trisk   Who's he?

Lika   I just told you. He's the landlord.

Trisk   His name.

Lika   Mister.

Trisk   His name is *Mister*?

Lika   Yes. Mister Deka D. (*Pause.*) Mister is his first name, and Deka –

Trisk   – Isn't.

Lika (*ignores the sarcasm*)   No. (*Pause.*) Mister Deka. (*Pause.*) With a 'D'.

Trisk   Mister *Deka*.

Lika   With a 'D'.

Trisk   'D' for?

Lika   D. (*Pause.*) Mister Deka D.

Trisk   He looks . . . Mister Deka D looks . . . clean.

Lika   He is – clean broke. Turned up on the front-step one morning sometime ago with not a penny to his name and said, 'Can I sit down for a moment?'

Trisk   And?

Lika   He sat down.

Trisk   Of course. Naturally. (*Pause.*) I thought you said he was a regular.

Lika   He was.

Trisk   I thought you said he owned the joint.

Lika   He did. But not any more.

Trisk   Who owns it now?

Lika   I haven't a clue. I only live here.

Trisk *takes a second look at* **Mister Deka D**.

Trisk   I know that face. (*Pause.*) It's *him*, isn't it?

Lika   Who?

Trisk   Him.

Lika   Who?

Trisk (*excitedly*)   Him!

Lika (*calmly*)   Who?

Trisk   In the papers. He was in the papers.

Lika   When?

Trisk   Then.

Lika   Maybe.

Trisk   Is it true?

Lika   What?

Trisk   That they struck him off?

Lika   When?

Trisk   He no longer operates?

Lika   Who?

Trisk (*nods at* **Mister Deka D**)   He's no longer a surgeon?

Lika *does not look up from her newspaper.*

Lika   They struck him off.

Trisk   Why?

Lika   They threw him out of the operating room and sent him straight down to the morgue.

Trisk   What, from cut-and-paste to cut-and-cover?

Lika   Yes, from surgeon to mortician. (*Pause.*) And you know what he found down at the morgue?

Trisk   The dead?

Lika   Death. He found death.

Trisk   You mean, same patients, and no change in their condition?

Lika   Don't be stupid. *Him.*

Trisk   *He* died at the morgue? (*Pause.*) He looks more drunk than dead to me.

Lika   Dead. Drunk. What's the difference?

Trisk   Is he drunk?

Lika   No.

Trisk   Is he dead?

Lika   No.

Trisk   Why's he all dressed up?

Lika   It's his birthday today.

Trisk   How old is he?

Lika   Several decades, a few years, several months, a few weeks and a day.

Trisk   So it isn't really his birthday today?

Lika   He holds every day to be his birthday.

Trisk   Why?

Lika   He counts the years one day at a time. I've known him to count them one moment at a time.

Trisk   Why? What's wrong with him?

Lika   He's dead drunk.

Trisk   I see.

Lika   He's always drunk.

Trisk   I see. (*Pause.*) Have you been out today?

Lika   No. Why?

Trisk   You need to go out more often.

Lika   Lovely weather today, wasn't it?

Trisk   Yes.

Lika   The sun was blazing.

Trisk   Yes.

Lika   It was amazing.

Trisk   Yes.

Lika   I prefer the moon myself.

Trisk   Why's that?

Lika   It comes out at night. *Pause.* How was the war?

Trisk   Terrific. It all went like a dream.

Lika   How many lives did you take?

Trisk   You mean, single-handedly? None.

Lika   None?

Trisk   None.

Lika   How many did you mangle?

Trisk   None.

Lika   None?

Trisk   None.

Lika   Was it –

Trisk   Great? Of course, it was. I was awarded a medal for bravery.

Lika   Why? What did you do to deserve a medal?

Trisk   When you're killing people, Lika, 'none' is more than enough.

The doorbell rings.

Silence.

It rings again.

Trisk *looks at* **Lika**.

Lika (*to* **Trisk**)   It's open. (*Shouts.*) Come in, the door is open.

They wait. Nobody comes in.

Pause.

Trisk (*continuing the interrupted conversation*)   And, hey, I'm here.

Lika   You're here.

Trisk   I'm back.

Lika   You're back.

Trisk   In one piece.

Lika   Nothing missing.

Trisk   Not a thing.

Lika   All in one piece.

Trisk (*stretches his arms*)   See? All mine. (*Stretches his feet.*) All mine. I'm back here, and still all there.

Lika   No close shaves?

Trisk   More than a few. (*Pause.*) I often thought that every moment was my next. But I saw no action.

Lika   None?

Trisk   None. Except for that one time when I ambushed an enemy.

Lika   You ambushed someone?

Trisk   I told you about it.

Lika   You did?

Trisk   You know I did, Lika. You know I did. (*Pause*) I wrote every day. (*Pause.*) Why did you never reply?

Lika *goes round the bar and fetches a bunch of letters, all sealed, tied together with a string.*

Lika   I never opened them.

Trisk   That's obvious.

Lika   I never thought you'd make it back.

Trisk   Obviously.

Pause.

Lika   I was, I suppose, already mourning.

Trisk (*bitterly*)   You could have read the letters *and* mourned just as well. (*Pause.*) Do you know how I consoled myself back there as the bullets flew around me?

Lika   How?

Trisk (*intones*)   'She hasn't replied, that's bad. But I know she's read it, *that's* good.' (*Pause.*) I have a healthy talent for self-assurance.

Pause.

Lika (*wryly*)   Don't I know that. You were telling me about the day you ambushed an enemy.

Trisk   Yes.

Lika   What happened?

Trisk   Nothing much. I shot him in the foot.

Lika   You shot him in the foot.

Trisk   Right in the foot. (*Indicates.*) Right here.

Lika   Did you mean to kill him?

Trisk   Of course.

Lika   You aimed to kill him.

Trisk   I did.

Lika   Why then did you aim for his foot? Why didn't you aim for his head?

Trisk   Someone else had already done that, with admirable precision.

Lika   He was already dead when you shot him in the foot?

Trisk   Yes.

Lika   And you knew this before you shot him in the foot?

Trisk   Yes.

Lika   And how did you feel after shooting him in the foot?

Trisk   Like a hero.

Lika   You felt like a hero.

Trisk   Yes. (*Pause.*) How else would you have me feel?

Lika   You felt like a hero after shooting a dead man in the foot?

Trisk (*heatedly*)   It was war, Lika, nothing personal.

Lika   You had orders.

Trisk   I had orders.

Lika   To shoot.

Trisk   I had orders to shoot.

Lika   It was war.

Trisk   Yes.

Lika   So you shot a dead man in the foot.

Trisk   Yes.

Lika   Why?

Trisk   It was him or me.

Lika   But he was already dead.

Trisk   Exactly. Think what I'd have had to do if he was alive.

Lika   Kill him?

Trisk   Of course. You see now, don't you, why I had to shoot him in the foot?

Lika   No.

Trisk (*exasperated*)   He was dead. There was no need to kill him twice. (*Pause.*) I need money. Lend me some money.

Lika   Is that why you're here, to ask for money? I thought you'd come for the party.

Trisk   What party?

Lika   Mister Deka D's party.

Trisk   Mister Deka D's having a party?

Lika   It's his birthday, remember? I thought that was why you were here.

Trisk   It is. But I need money.

Lika   For food? (You said you were hungry)

Trisk   No.

Lika   You're having trouble paying the mortgage?

Trisk   No.

Lika   You've exceeded your credit limit?

Trisk   No.

Lika   Your creditors are after you?

Trisk   No.

Pause.

Lika   Then why do you need to borrow from me?

Pause.

Trisk   I need to buy a car.

Lika   You can't keep a car if you haven't got money.

Trisk (*quietly*)   I need money, Lika, not advice.

Pause.

Lika   So you've become a father.

Trisk (*enthusiastically*)   Yes, Lika.

Lika   Boy or a girl?

Trisk   Yes, Lika. How did you know?

Lika   How?

Trisk   Yes, how?

Lika   How? How! How?! (How), how. (*She chokes. Coughs. Reaches for a glass of water, takes a sip and gradually recovers.*) She's late.

Trisk   How-who?

Lika *gestures at the vacant chair.*

Lika   She's always late.

Trisk   Does she know about the party?

Lika   What party?

Trisk   Mister Deka D's party.

Lika   *That.* No.

Trisk   Were you expecting her here today?

Lika   No.

Trisk (*with a grave shake of his head*)   She's always late.

Lika   Always.

Trisk   She's always late.

Lika   Always.

The doorbell rings. They ignore it.

Trisk   Yes.

Lika   Do you think – ?

Trisk   On the tube, yes.

Lika   That she got stuck on the tube?

The doorbell continues to ring. They ignore still. Finally, it stops ringing.

Lika   You're broke.

Trisk   Yes.

Lika   You need money?

Trisk   Yes.

Lika   You want me to lend you money?

Trisk   Yes.

Lika *stands up. She clenches her fist.*

Lika   I'll lend you all I've got if you can tell me what I've got in here.

Trisk   What, in your hand?

Lika   Yes.

Trisk   Simple: a submarine, a supermarket and a spaceship.

Lika *slaps him in the face.*

Trisk (*smarting, angry*)   Why did you do that?

Lika (*furious*)   You cheated.

Trisk   How?

Lika (*hurt*)   You must have seen me pick them up.

Lika *reaches for her purse and empties the contents, a few coins, on the table.* **Trisk** *does not touch them.*

There's a long silence.

In the silence, **Lika** *very quietly begins to weep, tears flow freely from her eyes.* **Trisk** *watches, confused, at first unsure what to do.*

Trisk   What's wrong, Lika? What's the matter?

He fetches a handkerchief from his pocket and hands it to her.

Lika (*wiping the tears off*)   Thanks, Trisk.

Trisk   Why were you crying?

Lika   No reason.

Trisk   No reason?

Lika   I do that from time to time.

Trisk   Why's that?

Lika   So when something terrible happens I don't have to cry.

Trisk   What do you do when something terrible happens?

Lika   I laugh.

Trisk   You laugh?

Lika   When I'm asked why I'm laughing, I say, didn't you see me weeping yesterday? I was weeping in credit. Now, leave me alone. Let me laugh in credit of happy days to come.

Trisk   So you weep when you're happy?

Lika (*emphatically, makes to say*)   No. I just pretend not to be impressed.

But, yet again, the loud drill, coming from the flat upstairs, suddenly comes on, drowning the conversation.

Lika *and* **Trisk** *continue talking. We watch their mouths move but cannot hear a single word of the spirited exchange.*

Not once during this scenario does either of them even look up to the ceiling or visually acknowledge the source of the noise.

Deka's *moronic grin is not one bit ruffled.*

The noise stops as suddenly as it began.

The silence catches **Lika** *and* **Trisk** *in mid-conversation.*

Or, rather, the silence meets with silence: **Lika** *and* **Trisk** *are holding what appears to be a heated conversation but, even as their lips move feverishly, no words come out of their mouths. They continue this mute exchange for quite a long while, then slowly lapse into total quietude.*

Trisk (*finally*)   What's that noise?

Lika   What noise?

Trisk   Can't you hear it?

Lika   Where?

Trisk   Listen.

They both listen intently.

Total silence.

Trisk   Hear that?

Lika (*with a sudden start*)   You mean *that*. (*Dismissively.*) That's my neighbour upstairs.

Trisk   You have a neighbour?

Lika   Yes.

Trisk   Upstairs.

Lika   Yes. (*Pause.*) She's meditating.

Trisk   Forgive me, Lika –

Lika   Why?

Trisk   I mean, I know I'm stupid –

Lika   You do?

Trisk   But *that* racket doesn't sound like meditation to me.

Lika   No?

Trisk   That sounds more like someone using a giant drill to assault a wall.

Lika   That's what she's doing.

Trisk   She's drilling a hole in a wall?

Lika (*nods*)   That's how she meditates.

Trisk   Really? And what's this form of meditation called?

Lika   Reverse-yoga.

Trisk   Reverse-yoga?

Lika   That's what she calls it.

Trisk   *Reverse-yoga?*

Lika (*nods*)   She's becoming something of guru. Her message is catching on fast.

Trisk   What exactly is her message?

Lika   When you've got noisy neighbours, don't get even – get drilling.

Trisk   That's her message?

Lika   That's her message. She had a vision.

Trisk   She's a psycho . . . I mean, psychic?

Lika   She's written a book about it. *Drilling to Happiness*, it's called.

Trisk   Have you read it?

Lika   Not yet. But I've heard her read bits of it to the neighbours. It starts with her theory of how we all got here. Her theory of what happened in the hour of none.

Trisk   The hour of none?

Lika   That's what she calls it. What Happened in the Hour of None.

Trisk   And how it happened?

Lika   And how it happened.

Trisk   And why it happened?

Lika   And why it happened.

Trisk   And where it happened?

Lika (*nods*)   And when.

Trisk   Point by point?

Lika   And straight from the heart. Would you like to hear it?

Pause.

It all started once upon a time when day and night did not exist, when the past, the present and the future were one, when eternity was but a moment and a moment seemed like for ever. Time was a great fish – bigger than the highest mountains and, sometimes when it had a mind to it, smaller than a speck of dust. It lay asleep at the bottom of an ice-rock ocean, heaving its giant-midget gills every once in a billion light years, or even twice in the blink of a fluttering eye. The universe shook when it breathed. Non-existent galaxies echoed its sighs. And the earth was birthed from the trickle of saliva that dripped from its jaws. When it awoke and took to flight, it *thought* clouds into being. And when it dived out from the very bowels of the earth and soared into the sky, its wings were the very clouds it had thought into existence. Its wings stretched out from one end of the earth to the other, ending where they began and beginning where they ended. It remained motionless when it moved and could not be stopped even when it stood still. It was a huge creature, this great fish that flew into the sky. Its heart was everywhere and its body, its huge, endless body, unfolded and was countless in its parts, like the specks of sand in a desert or the cluster of stars in all galaxies or the sum-total of all thoughts in all minds from all time in all beings. It created the sun to warm its back, and the moon to caress its stomach. It lay with the sun, and day was born. It lay with the moon, and night was born. Day was lonely, and so was night. Day and night, the first children, played together in a nursery of nothingness and to stay their boredom, named toys into being. They named sound, and sound existed. They named sight, and sight existed. They named other things, and reality was born. And reality, lonely from the start, named morning and noon as well and evening too, and the days of the week, and the weeks of the year, and eternity and a month, and an hour of minutes and a millennium in seconds and these all came into being. And they in turn named the denizens of the sea, and the inhabitants of the land, and the creatures of the air, and these too came into being. And the world, in all its ugly-beauty, was born.

Pause.

Trisk (*quietly*)   'And the world was born.' (*Long silence.*) But what does it, you know, what does it . . . ?

Lika   It *doesn't*. (*Pause.*) It *is*.

Trisk (*dismayed*)   It just *is*? Surely, it must be . . . surely, there must be, surely, an equals-*to* that it's *equals*-to? Surely, Lika, surely.

Lika   It's equals-to *its* equals-to.

Trisk   It's equal *to* its equal?

Lika   Yes.

Trisk (*confused, hesitantly*)   Which is to say –

Lika   It equals its equal.

Trisk (*taking it in*)   It . . . equals its equal?

Lika   Yes.

Pause.

Trisk   Which is?

Lika   You.

Trisk (*perplexed*)   It's equals-to *me*?

Lika   And me. And this and that. And that or the other. And you and me.

Trisk   I'll drink to that. (*He drinks.*) To you and me.

Lika   It equals to you and me. (*Pause.*) It equals-to the first time we met. Was it spring? Was it summer? Was it autumn, was it winter? I don't remember now.

Trisk   (I do. It was raining like . . . I don't know what, but it was.)

Lika   It equals-to the day you left, when you walked out that door, when you turned round and said to me,

Trisk   'Are you sure that's what you want?'

Lika   And I said, 'Yes, go away. Don't come back.' (*Pause.*) No, Trisk, that's not how it happened. That isn't what happened. What happened was this: I said to you, 'Are you sure that's what you want?' You said to me, 'Yes, I'm going away and I'm not coming back.'

Trisk (*heatedly*)   That's not true. That's not how it happened. That's simply not true.

Lika   It wasn't spring that day, or summer or autumn or winter. It was simply the day you went your way and I went mine. (*Pause.*) Where did you go? (*Pause.*) Why are you back?

Trisk   I went for a walk. I fought in a war. I took long rides on the tube. I met someone new. We had a child. She met someone new. The seasons changed. I changed with the seasons. I was out on a walk tonight. I came down this street, I walked past this address, Number 1, 2, 3, 4 and 5, your lights were on, I turned round and came to your door, I rang the bell, you let me in. That's why I'm here. (*Pause.*) I was out on a walk tonight. I came down this street, I walked past this address, Number 1, 2, 3, 4 and 5, your lights were on, I turned round and I came to your door, I rang the bell, the door was open, I walked inside. And there you were.

Lika   And there I was. (*Quietly.*) The party is over, Trisk.

Trisk   What party?

Lika   You keep forgetting it's Mister Deka D's birthday party. It was a great party, wasn't it?

Trisk   Fabulous. We must do it again.

Lika   Yes.

Pause.

Trisk   When?

Lika   I don't know. Soon.

Trisk   Soon? Are you sure? (*Pause.*) Is that spoken from the heart?

Lika   I- I don't know, Trisk.

Trisk (*hurriedly*)   That's all right. Soon's good enough for me. (*Pause.*) Soon . . . that's soon . . . enough. (*He gets up.*) Well, I'd better be going now.

Lika   How will you get home?

Trisk   I'll catch a night bus. I may even walk back.

Lika   Back where?

Trisk   There.

Lika   Where's 'there'?

Trisk   Where I live.

Lika   Which is where?

Trisk   No, it isn't.

Lika   It isn't what?

Trisk   It isn't where.

Lika   What isn't where?

Trisk   Isn't it?

Lika   You know it isn't.

Trisk   Well, I don't live there.

Lika   But you just said you did.

Trisk   Where?

Lika (*shakes her head*)   No, there.

Trisk   That's right.

Lika   Where's that?

Trisk   I don't know.

Lika   You don't know where you live?

Trisk (*with mild indignation*)   Of course I do. I just told you a minute ago.

Lika (*takes a deep breath*)   Let's start again. Where do you live?

Trisk   There.

Lika   Where's 'there'?

Trisk   Not too far from here.

Pause.

Lika *picks up the money on the table and presses it into his hand.*

Lika   Here, take a cab.

Trisk (*brushes it aside, laughs*)   No, Lika. I prefer the night bus.

Lika   You do? You used to hate it.

Trisk   I don't any more. I like the way it wings its way slowly but steadily across the streets at night, just like the ferry across the ocean of existence. It gives me time to think.

Lika   'The ferry across the ocean of existence?'

Trisk   Time.

Pause.

Trisk *searches briefly for something.*

Lika   What have you lost?

Trisk (*spots his shoes on his feet*)   Ah, there they are. I knew I'd brought them with me. Did I tell you what my mother used to say about shoes?

Lika   Yes.

Trisk   She said to me, 'Son, always wear your shoes. That's what they're there for.'

Lika   That's what she said?

Trisk   Honest to – (*Sneezes.*) Straight from the – (*Sneezes.*)

They make to hug, then stop short.

Exit **Trisk**.

She watches him leave.

A long pause.

Mister Deka D *snaps awake, in a panic, as if from a nightmare.*

Mister Deka D (*shouting*)   Where I am?

Lika (*wearily*) Here.

Mister Deka D   That's where?

Lika   Number 1, 2, 3, 4 and 5.

Mister Deka D   Number 5, 4 . . . Where on that's earth?

Lika   Here. Right here.

Mister Deka D   'Right here.' Is the *Z to A* on the that? Tell me there to get how.

Lika   You don't need the *A to Z*, Mister Deka D. This is it. Here.

Mister Deka D (*looks round*)   Here?

Lika   Here. It's not out there somewhere, Mister Deka D. It's right here.

Mister Deka D (*dubiously*)   Here?

Lika   Right here, Mister Deka D. You're standing in it.

Mister Deka D   Here? No bout adoubt it?

Lika   No doubt about it, Mister Deka D. This is it. Number 1, 2, 3, 4 and 5.

Mister Deka D (*suddenly grins*)   I'm not so think as you drunk I am.

Lika   I don't quite follow, Mister Deka D.

Mister Deka D (*recites*)
  For example, to prove it I'll tale you a tell –
  I once knew a fellow named Apricot –

I'm sorry, I just chair over a fell –
A trifle – this chap, on a very day hot –
If I hadn't consumed that last whisky of tot! –
As I said now, this fellow, called Abraham –
Ah? One more? Since it's you! Just a do me will spot –
But I'm not so think as you drunk I am.

The doorbell rings. They let it ring for a while.

Lika (*finally*)   It's open. (*Shouts, exasperated.*) My door's
open.

Mister Deka D (*grimly*)   I've got a serious make to
complaint, Lika.

Lika   What is it, Mister Deka D?

Mister Deka D   It's . . . afraid . . . I'm . . . rather grave,
It's . . . in allegation . . . an fact. (*Pause.*) It's come to my
forgotten that you've attention something important today,
Lika.

Lika   That's it? It's come to your attention that I've
forgotten something important? That's the allegation?

Mister Deka D   Yes, is it.

Lika   Who made this allegation, Mister Deka D?

Pause.

Mister Deka D (*grimly, resolutely*)   I, Lika, I'm that
alligator.

Pause.

Lika (*sings*)
  Happy birthday to you.
  Happy birthday to you.
  Happy birthday, Mister Deka D,
  Happy birthday to you.

Mister Deka D *breaks into a huge grin.*

The doorbell continues to ring.

Slow fade until **Mister Deka D***'s face, captured in a halo, is all we see.*

Pause.

Blackout.